T0078698

As
I Z

Books

Howell (Atelos Books, 2011)

The Adventures of Pi (Dos Madres Press, 2011)

The Hero Project of the Century (The Backwaters Press, 2009)

On Spec (Omnidawn Publishing, 2008)

c.c. (Krupskaya Books, 2002)

Chapbooks

Trump l'oeil (Hostile Books, 2017)

Between Red and Green: Narrative of the Black Brigade
(Dos Madres Press, 2016)

Red Between Green (Portable Press @Yo-Yo Labs, 2015)

Pink Tie (Hooke Press, 2011)

Musique Noir (Overhere Press, 2006)

Futures, Elections (Dos Madres, 2004)

AAB (Slack Buddha Press, 2004)

Tyrone Williams/Taylor Brady: Segue Reading Series
(A Rest Press, Ltd. Edition, 2003)

Convalescence (poems), (Ridgeway Press, 1987,
2nd printing 1989; 3rd printing 1994)

As Iz

TYRONE WILLIAMS

OMNIDAWN PUBLISHING
OAKLAND, CALIFORNIA
2018

© Copyright Tyrone Williams, 2018
All rights reserved.

Cover art by Jill Magi: "Bone, Version I" (back), watercolor, acrylic, graphite, plywood, 61 x 61 cm;
and "Bone, Version 4" (front), paper, acrylic, graphite; 57 x 76 cm.

Interior image:
"I AM A MAN" © Dr. Ernest C. Withers, Sr.,
WITHERS FAMILY TRUST

Cover typeface: Letter Gothic Std, Warnock Pro, Adobe Jenson Pro
Interior typeface: Adobe Jenson Pro

Cover & interior design by Cassandra Smith

Offset printed in the United States
by Thomson-Shore, Dexter, Michigan
On 55# Enviro Natural 100% Recycled 100% PCW
Acid Free Archival Quality FSC Certified Paper

Library of Congress Cataloging-in-Publication Data

Names: Williams, Tyrone, author.
Title: As iZ / Tyrone Williams.
Description: Oakland, California : Omnidawn Publishing, 2018.
Identifiers: LCCN 2018014072 | ISBN 9781632430618 (pbk. : alk. paper)
Classification: LCC PS3573.I456137 A85 2018 | DDC 811/.54--dc23
LC record available at https://lccn.loc.gov/2018014072

Published by Omnidawn Publishing, Oakland, California
www.omnidawn.com (510) 237-5472 (800) 792-4957

10 9 8 7 6 5 4 3 2 1

ISBN: 978-1-63243-061-8

ACKNOWLEDGMENTS

Many of these poems were first published in various print and online journals and magazines. I want to thank the editors of the following: *A Perimeter*, *Aufgabe*, *The Baffler*, *The Bathhouse Journal*, *Chicago Review*, *The Elderly*, *Eleven Eleven*, *The Harvard Advocate*, *Hambone*, *Jacket*, *MAKE*, *[out of nothing]*, *Spiral Orb*, *Virginia Quarterly Review*, and *The Volta*.

"To the future Master Charlie Rebel" was written for the late Benjamin Hollander who collated the collection *Letters for Olson*.

Table of Contents

To Market

LIBRARY

This book is dedicated to the thinking

of Chandra Talpade Mohanty and Jalal Toufic.

Wizard of Mot-

          ley rag-
tag-no-
yo'-you-
it-in-
teamdom-cum-tin
              ear
fraidy fraidy
line
       scare
       quotes [cf.
tora tora]
tori
       [Miz Spelling 2
           u-
turn blutopic in
toto
tort low
yella
          iz
wee way
of dis
off-shore a-
ccount of dragged water-

                    mark
wee wear an extra
e-
            [rrant spelling
de-masks de
masked
            humongous
                    homunculus
clad in hiz-
sonner's green
red Office
19Good
                Witch
Bad War-
locked-
            in
                Dot
                    period
aperiodic
piece b&w
color color
b&w-cast
                [cf. J.F.K.,
The Hindenburg,
et al]
            /fast
            pix-

ie

/els

     cursor

        pre-

cursor

w[h]*iz-

zened

mot[e]**

*As these **three disastrous asterisks subtend, the function of this h, this e, is to demarcate, border, separate, Egypt, for example, from Judah (to say nothing of Israel), magic from miracle, etc., even if the integration of these supposed antipodes remains essential to all the tribunes and tributaries of Judaism and Islam (to say nothing of Christianity).

Pharmacy

"Poisons and medicine are often the same substance given with different intents."—Peter Mere Latham, 19th-century English physician and educator

occident, n. "not of the essence, insubstantial, error, errancy"—from *The Dictionary of the Forthcoming Caliphate*

Serapis

A dead gods, one
good descends from Concord,
one, St. Louis, the Spirit
to follow (a third one
having gone before)
leaps within a womb
where it sits at the feet
of the formula of chance:

$$\frac{x}{y}$$

the in one
thesis is a response to,
response from, a call—
When I fish in Hegel
I cannot get a bite—

nothing other than the skeletal
remains save the Concord
School of Philosophy, a bust
crowned with measured corn
leaps within a tomb,
a scheme to rhyme birth
and death, to track *living*

tissue, upright and bent
to drink from a water fountain
as an algebra of stars,
dragged through the streets,
dismembers into simple

division

Hear You Who Abandon Here Ye

The wildcat strikes—"other minds"—
foreclose on future unbroken circles, replacement arcs,
debris field over a new mount.

´ `

This cis-
star myth
of occluded Being:
acute disaster
grave catastrophe

      stand on, in,
           for
the dead letter
run aground
      is a sundial
      raised to clock
a darkish hue—
      gold
      emerald
      bronze
      silver
      lead
      topaz
      tin—
of crushed blue
lips kissed
by crux ax
      and atop,

the toppled

at rest

at the feet of heart and feather.

Syrian Wheel

for Mel Chin

The noise abatement procedures of the book amount to a levee
banked at the edges of a floodplain, the elevation, if not apotheosis, of
case law to the spoke-eye axis around which a world revolves, passing
through that on which it is mounted: standard-issue trousers and
jeans, dress shoes and cas-Fridays. Set into motion by Rapid Finger
Movement, the dream of propulsion is as real as the Doppler Effects
of approaching and receding horizons, a dreaming without which the
edifice capsizes, and washed ashore, dries out as a newly-baptized
scaffold for a sun disk, sundial or, per shrinkage, Frisbee.

Serapeum (Domestic)

In this shotgun apartment among primitive cumulus every cat,
however neutered, can cut loose: cut noses, cut notes, cut back
against the rush to the edge, cut to the net over a hole, and so on.
And so we pounce upon the Cloud, roll around in pillowy ideograms:
Michael, LeBron, Beyonce, Sanders, Ohio State, Michigan, the
Allmans, Foghat, Jimi, etc. Cats chasing light, darting here, there,
reflection of some watch, ring, or cufflinks, we play, cool as cucumbers
in the vegetable bin. And then someone, something, somehow cuts to
the chase: a blast of cold air—the wreckage of rupture aloft we peek
outside: one day we all will speak Mandarin and Urdu/ or "a couple
of nukes will take care of that." This close to the fire daylighting a sky
my watch says otherwise. According to which, what are we still doing
up?

Sky—

_____

isn't it,
i.e.,
e.g.   excludes
itself
invisible middle
nothing—not
the bone of Buraq
sans Icarus
not the spirit
of Pegasus
de Rocinante
not a stopped-up
aromathematics
[Abraham minus jihad
        ||
animal plus sacrifice]
not a bold
aperitif *ex machina*—
can de-fulcrum
idée fixe
planes the flat
air to a
fine finish.

We See The Sky And Raise It

Perdream to have sent
And resent as recent as
Tomorrow a thumb
Piano   text

At risk per se—
Abbreviated ash—iotas
Cast as shadows
Cast no spells—

Orange cones   curtain rods—
Demselves spelled by them
Faith in faster-than-father travel
As though through travail

(hysterical glass)
Blue declensions
Vanish into A-
Velocity.

See Above

Indebted to the general
displacement of ground
                    sky horizon the
decimated ranks of one
thousand and one
                    Arabian midnights
conscripted into children
drowning in the Mirror
                    Loch of conscious-
ness can no longer be
said to −scend or −scend
                    turn −wise or −wise
Ezekiel's mis-
spoken wheel.
                    Persia aside...
frames the rabid
virgins-sirens
                    frothing up the Dead
Sea. Bound disaster
the horn of plenty
                    replenishes his
captive crew to say
nothing of the coffins-
                    coffers below: exhibit
A of case no.
ur- and Third
                    on permanent loan-

continuance to Franco-
Anglo-phone museums-

                    nations at competitive
rates unspelled out
being the given

                    groundlessness a-
cross which a pigeon-toed
bow-legged abomination—

                    Big Foot—
amortizes fe-
fi-fo-fum *trés*-

                    passer-by and by *bien*

Sphinx Infinitives

Here—ahead-
a first cross-
dressing humanimal

an index finger over the lips of God,
                                    pursed
sleight-of-smile
a bow suspended
above the bridge

overture to an overture
                                    bent slight.

Here looms
raised brow
heir to heir-

loom and 'fro the sweat-

tomb of the unknown slave

where for every Khafre work
there will have been a Khulu work-
                                    shop chopped

                    off

ankh *sans* an
- -

Tunisia, Tunisia, wherefore art, Tunisia?

Dizzy chicken
                careens skyward
        squawk ex-*x*
where for every exuberant *here!* hear
                ye/you—
string instrument of the middle finger
                excluded

Morocco-pressed into service elevates Egypt—
                        revolver with a rifle scope
abases Syria—
                        revolving v. reinforced fire-
doors/power—
Unmoved.

So moved:
Hor-Em-Ahket
is to be, the

                motion, having passed,

inflates to
as it wards
off-peak *ad*

                hoc olfactum

TB

A
player to be named
later the history did it
                did us in out of dick
bird copper envy
                did us in in I I
capital trade-
decapitated wise-
                guys made head-
way with some tail-
                wind spooked
                air harp
blown like a save or
                        plucked
                        out of tin
iron yen Saud Asia
Minor
                                        *   *   *

 Belaborated
                                *   *   *

Chicken is the game—the chicken is game
                                *   *   *

(aside) the book
        sotto voce

                screen-swept
Windows treatments broken

                vessel
                an an-
                eurysm
preempts the offstage

                feed
                the dead
                link
dragged like a lake

                front A-
                dobe
                Reader
the talkies won't sing

                                        wing it

Inmate

Driven by imaginal gut bacteria a taxicab driver goes rogue from the standstill traffic of rush hour, pulling off onto the shoulder of the freeway. He exits the vehicle as ordered, free tenor with a prayer rug, spreads it out upon the gravel, falls to his knees, and amid the fumes of gasoline, tar and oil, the cacophony of blaring horns, squealing brakes, and rumbling mufflers, begins his ministrations to the brains.

Between the Gap Unlike 12 and 30

Nothing—not-
to-be-never-was. His
"I" passing
for, through, an
"eye of" A
"needle," the
doorway without a
door, an
anagram surpassing
disaster, his
they know not

what they do—not,
as we know, his
per se, but sayings passed
down by mouth, an
oral procedure, a
transfiguration of the
body of work, a
gift from, to, an
in the spirit of, unsurpassed
play of our lapses, his
unaccounted for, dilemmas not

unlike the gap between 12 and 30.

The Gazarene

He kneels still, statu-
esque in Gethsemane, E-
gypt passing to, fro-

m, between him, u-
xorious aroma, o-
lives not pressed, not oil.

bBaraka

I.

Take a seat, says b to B, the flat plane
of instruction a tier above the floor of worship,

though from a bird's nest swaying side to side with prejudice,
the shore is both the start and end of water—then land—

and every seat's an ottoman if one envisions
another seat, nearby, one with backing, and so, a chair,

or just a seat in fact, or stoop reduced to just
a seat, in brief, a seat that's only a step not taken,

one's feet planted firmly on ground. Moreover,
b and B beside each other seem to themselves

to typify the difference between floor and tier
as one of scale, and scale, scaffold. Be flat

and not sums up inhuman music, shifting earth,
solid states dissolving into middle stages.

II.

Because and despite the dark ages of Jahiliyyah,
slow- and fast-moving waters deposit erosion

and meander means down, south and sideways blues
impulse if not the blues of the current serpent-

serpentine heresies the play of eddies and backwaters.
Nothing escapes the black holes of Congo Square

and Mecca but the breakdances of the prophets
and the homage-parody of whirling dervishes.

The Gregorian call to prayer frees jazz to over
sky and under burqa the middle left to board

III.

New Ark. To stand, in short, behind a throne
as nomadic camels kneel into neighbors

and contagion marked as neighborhood takes root
and roots beget rumors of trunks at first, the trunk

at last becomes, at bottom, tree. To return
to forests hidden from the eye is thus to see

invisible ink streaming across a scroll of upheaval,
branches as the upper promise of roots. And stars

cast as site-specific installations mean
jihadist texts v. jihadist contexts. b,

says B, rising to his feet, time to step
off, and off he goes, a tangent to the scaffold

and its ground, a third vector of many ways,
masked crusader, the hijab in his wake repurposed cape.

e ë

The stained-glass windows of a police station as seen from behind
and between the bars of a cell?

Done. What else you got?

The glass partition behind which a technician stands as a little bang
explodes inside a chest as a new universe?

Check. And?

Central air convectors as curatives for heliophilia?

Right. Next?

Concavity of cone and plane, 911 operators standing by to take all
parables since this is only an arch emergency?

Tried that—couldn't hit the curve.

Hijabberwocky pregnant with a blank burqa, disownment a cord to
be cut at both ends?

Got it,

and so the imperial dream of three cultures veils,

for one, a fourth (at least), preeminent sediment:

Capetanis' Toletum, Toletum's Capetani

who return from error as others of themselves,

and two by two walk between the Styx and Styx,

ahead, a new Toledo, beyond, Hamtramck anew.

∧

for eLSeed and Tyree Guyton

\

…nor *this tent* that *is not a tent*
of bed sheet cardboard overpass

or tie-dyed house enjambing dolls
neither a colorized pyramid of sabots—

the right sound shoehorned into the wrong note—

nor the little hat of some untouched-up coolie
neither a pile of books outside abandoned showers—

point is, the road not taken is thereby taken

/

The east side of Detroit is no more East Detroit
than it is *the place of combat,* pockmarked
with shoeprints as the absence of shoes, if not feet

East Detroit is no more not Detroit
than the city of a thousand minarets
encompasses the neighborhood Garbage City—

the right odor being music, the palate's palette—

The traffic in spices bypassed the mother of the world,
went south to circumnavigate the Cape of Good
Hope—the two bridges (not) of Cairo Ill.—

site-defeated as railroad cash saws its coffin—

Now New Cairo renders Cairo Old
Cairo, and Old Cairo, wrapped in a stole
of calligraphy, the perfume of *belles lettres*,

strikes a pose for its close-up from Mt. Mokattam

p.s. ..

an eraglass flipped by real estate lords
it over the clocks above the city hall of glass
as if the mosque southwest of the city border wagged

Alhambra

To be seen and not
heard, herded, and yet,
heralded—ambidoxic
harem, primary colors-studded
headdress, cross-stitched
veil over hollowed-out.

taškïl

A musky woman,

disappeared into "the Fragrant Concubine,"

finds her legs

shedding the shroud of her grandfather's mausoleum,

steps out

into a new Kashgar,

the old city.

Uyghur rubble under Han redevelopment

remains discernible

in the smell of her body bathed in camel milk,

in her bowlegged gait,

two-legged chair draped in out of date clothes

sidling sashaying

like the beast that once bore her to Beijing

where a Qianlong emperor

wooed her with her own charms in miniature

replicas of her village

garden, mosque and oasis, a splash of cow milk

in her tea.

Earthbound over

hidden from Uyghur and Han eyes

a grape

on the tongue of the last imam

a gift

not unlike the last gift

from the emperor

jujube tree

and won over to the consolation of poison-

tipped daggers sheathed in festooned sleeves

slashed her torso

cut so straight it might have served as a second mouth

shut wide save

viscera revealed.

To Market

To market, to market, to buy a penny bun,

Home again, home again, market is done.

—traditional English nursery rhyme

1. International

To the future Master Charlie Rebel,

among the *topoi* of our Lord, 1630

Now, reduced to here, this island, discrete, I myself am only I, a
thwarted man. Petition after petition to go abroad, to return to the
new world I christened New England (I dream, of course, of that day
when it will be necessary to rename this spit of land New Britain)
for our King (yes, yours too, that pinnacle of divine right you keep
trying to flatten into your, as our, manifest destiny), rejected, denied.
So I write, for what else can a de-sailed man do? Yes, I am reduced
to a man of letters, the humiliation of the desk and sitting-room.
I presume you will have known, and doubtless will have despised,
Tennyson's "Ulysses," that house-weary paean to our all-too-soon
waning empire (an ache I feel even though I stand on the other
side of the bell curve, in ascension). I get it, and though you sit—
no, stand—awashed in the glorious light of broken and conflated
humors, not unlike your presumptuous United States of America,
the genetic flaw, your mortal coil upon itself, has become, shall we
posit, rather visible. I know something about this, am told, have
heard, they claim, am too familiar.

And so, I am family, one of your ancestors, if not a relative. I
remain flattered to be claimed as one of your heroes. You understand,
then, the necessity of conquest, the annexation of spatiality by
space, one manifold of departure and destination as here we stand.
Yes, I too have toppled the tyranny of metaphor, imprisoned it in
the cells of my poems. However, I am disturbed by reports from

the future prior to yours, this Riemann and his influence on, if not over, you. Yes, I managed to map important sections of the land I dubbed New England. But this mapping, however technical, could not be abstracted into the mathematical idealisms that you derived from Riemannian geometry. This is hardly a defense of Euclid, that other genius of idealism. The earth is neither round nor flat; nor is it a sphere even if it approaches the spherical. You cast out the chimera of metaphor only to sneak it back in under the cover of metonym, a maximum contiguity cobbled together as a metaphysics of materialism. There is, in your various essays on "the getting rid" of this and that, a letting-in that comes or stands between the typewriter and thing, that is, an invited company of things that stand between one thing and another thing. Perhaps this is all due to this thing you dub "literature," which you scorn as that which interferes with what is before us, what can be apprehended by the musket, by the force of speech, though I have found, in my limited experience, nothing gets through the muck like a good sound thrashing...

By then you will have heard the rumors, the alleged mutiny, insurrection, and totalitarianism which I will not deny to you, my brother to come. I confess to these acts but not to their criminalization. For I crossed the sea with a ship of fools, a stiff-necked horde dressed up as "crew" and "passengers." Were it not for me you and your States would not exist. I apologize for nothing, I do not regret, do not look back, put one foot in front of another as I march into the annals which will have chronicled my journeys. You understand a man like me, a man who gets things done, the petty mores and customs of little minds notwithstanding. We are never not at war, and yet my expeditions which demanded the sacrifice of men are used to punish me as though I am to be held accountable for losses without compensations for the gains. I am held up as an "example," penned within the stockade of a people whose very survival remained perilous but for my interventions. What is at issue is neither the events nor their sequence but only the question of interpretation, how these markers are to be held—or if you will, published—as history. I won, triumphed over adversity, raised my savage countrymen to the highest pitch of possibility, and yet, though I put down this history, this mapping, in my own books, they have been overwritten by the envious and poisonous pens of my enemies. I trust you will provide the remedy for these injustices, these bloated travesties, the likes of which are truly unparalleled in the history of our—pardon me, my—great land.

I am once again asea, but this time I have no deck below me, no men around me. I spend my days writing letters to Her Majesty, letters that, I know, go unread, or if read, are scorned, tossed aside as I have been discarded, decommissioned. Usurped by scribblers who write of the savages with no direct knowledge of their habits and customs, who guess at the circumference of seas, rivers, lakes by sight alone, I am bereft, my attention to the particulars of coastal erosion, tidal eddies, reduced to pedantry. You too will suffer this fate, your incompetence at chair-sitting and bluster exposed in all its nakedness, what will be your Big Horn. Call it Black Rock.

Your humble brother,

Captain John Smith

Passing Goods

Primitive accumulations begin as annexations
sentimentalized as abandonment in latter days,
land as land for, for water toward land,
a staged decree née climate change, territorialized
exodus, a theatrical complex alchemical denominations:
history, psychology, as dialogue aside,
property per props, death-throes as method acting,
etc., woven into plots.

                    In each act,
as in each case, utter is a limit of failed,
accomplished genitives. Gerunds calcify,
spectacles loaded into magazines, magazines
loaded into machine guns, and guns—abandon,
abandoned by, machines—unload themselves,
relief felt, if not heard, around a world
failing description.

["_____in whom I am well pleased"]

                    A blow-up over England
during the Battle of Britain, Joseph K. mourns his losses
as he folds his many-vested coat into a future

castle repaired beyond the tower at Sandycove,

and dreaming of the sloppy wet kisses between national whiskey

and international waters, surveys the Celtic and Atlantic Seas.

"It was easy—

they sank my boat,"
quips the future
free world leader
downplaying
the Harvard man
as war hero
who did not go
down with the starboard
aft but clung
to the floating
wreckage with other
survivors led
to follow his wake
when he swam
out of the Blackett
Strait to Ferguson
Passage towing
a wounded crewman
with his teeth
until they reached
Olasana
as castaways
for six days
before the seventh when

Solomon Islanders
rescued them
a tale teeming
with peril
and redemption
just as Joseph
had hoped when he
pulled a few strings
to get a stringer
to play up
the harrowing ordeal
of his second son
that next to next
last chance
a backstory
buried at sea
with the actual
Pequod Torpedo
Boat 109
resurrected
as a replica
of the future
inaugural ask
not parade
end quote.

Charon on the Potomac

A cornered

stamp is a

dangerous

coin value

driven up

as it is

driven to

the brink of

extinction

not unlike

this conceit

by dint of

displacement

the lesser

abasement

compared to

akinship

with the coins

I retrieve

from the shades

of cold lips   to   the land of

or wet tongues   of the dead   the living

as my fee   deck to plie   from the land   reader a

for transport   this river   mocking

to the land   or carry   reversal
  of the dead   envelopes   though this thin
    demeans me   difference
      to a stamped   between the
        stamp that mans   same tenor
        all hands on   and different

                                            vehicles
                                    makes all the
                                      difference—
                                    proxy per
                                    permanence...

or so I'd hoped, resigned to middle management
by the reinforced ceiling of a vaulted Al-Araf, rumors
that it divides nothing from nothing notwithstanding.
I envied no plant, animal or human as long as my
not unimportant role in the play of existence was acknowledged
by those forms of being closest to ours and my name inspired

dread by those who profess faith that death is not oblivion.
But now as I recall those spheres, domes and temples, vain
aspirants to a glory that once populated the sky née heavens,
the vainglories of this capital Capitol offend me
and more, the national—no, epochal—reduction of me to a
children's story cannot, and will not, go unpunished however

much I lack the authority to impose my substantial powers.
At least that strange hunter I once saw standing on the veranda
of his mansion—yet another bow to vanity—near the land
these Americans named Mt. Vernon seemed to actually see me
for I recognized the sudden terror in his eyes. I smiled with pleasure
as I sailed by with another shipment of red, white and black savages.

Would that his descendants were as humble as they stroll
about dipping cups into their rivers of museums,
archives, libraries, memorials. Had I the power I'd
bend that National Harbor atrocity, Capital Wheel, into a
terrible train of gondolas plunging down the rapids of an agitated
Acheron into my waiting arms, a sneer widening into a maw.

Melinde Melindi

Abu al-Fida's written account of Melinde follows
tracks the Galana River to its mouth, sound

ledger on/in which the Pillar of Vasco da Gama
balances, is balanced by, Mount Kenya, vector

per vector as a credit/debt, correct/error,
edifice before lapsing into a common era

of undisturbed foliage and feral menagerie
encrypt Jesus Mohammed, arrest Christ the Prophet

until Sultan Majid pulls back the stone to enslave
Melinde's corpse and order Melindi's release

into a British protectorate as one—absent oil,
gold, etc.—chosen and resigned to a tourist resort

overlooking the Indian Ocean empty of pirate
trawlers, merchant ships and freighters steering clear

of the hidden scarecrows of Somali piracy
filling the nets of Kenyan fishermen

with the bounty of repopulated waters

cleansed in the absence of barges dumping waste.

defectiva/ plena

A maritime disputation
concerning the meeting-place of
two territorial waters
understood as directed by
the vector of a border
(Somalia) or perpendicular
to a coastline in accordance
with latitude and longitude
per international law
(Kenya). The inability to resolve has had an
impact on resolving peripheral issues, in particular, the
determination of economic
v. contiguous zones and the
distribution of mineral,
biological and national
rights. The impasse imperils both
countries' ability "to sell
exploration blocks and to collect
revenue from any subsequent
discoveries," a reference
to oil and gas deposits found
off the coasts of Tanzania
Mozambique. Hence capital
investments have been postponed,

stalling the development of

schools, hospitals, and beachfront

properties, to say nothing of

badly needed water treatment

facilities and medicines

to curtail the spread of water-

borne diseases however great

the risk of proliferating

endocrine disruptors as

miscisgenation.

Xcedilla

The soft sales of distance—tele-, email,
text, post—augur revenues lower
than those projected by prevailing
sentiment, the philosophical minds
of first responders: hands-on on-site likes.
Nevertheless, the value of distance—
l/l axis that corners the market—
climbs into a car already crowded
with service refugees seeking civic
and moral credit as the victims
of natural phenomena absorbed
as human disaster ad lib off script
and crawl, walk or run guns out of the frame,
retrofit lifeboats with rebuilt motors
powerful enough to chase down big game
out in the trade lanes of the Indian Ocean.
As for Waaq, Allah, Yahweh,
and God—names for the earthquake off the coast
of Sumatra, for the tsunami sent
to wipe out the lives and livelihoods
of coastal fishermen far from Xarardheere
where Range Rovers packed with televisions,
mattresses, computers, and furniture
race out of town ahead of believers
armed with *haram* but short on cash.

In the Wake of a Storm to Come

Outbreak jets of the British Empire, part
scramble for Africa,

                    part passenger pigeons
                    blocking the sun for days

on end before blue sky
cast as overhead

                    against pieces of the Horn
                    cost flotsam

in the Gulf and Ocean—

                    makeshift scows

adrift

                    in one, Geeska

        nods off,

                        chewing *khat*

wading through dreams of PT boats,

his fishing pole

the rod of Moses,

big-fish in the desert

jerk on the line

Geeska jerks

awake, intent,

breakfast

and if he's lucky

breakfast

tomorrow

for one man

a moment

no father

shot dead by Hart Security

guards

no grandfather

languishing in some overseas prison

for trying to jumpstart the Fisheries Protection Agency

no freighters on the
horizon

flat as a floe from the Nansen shelf

just Geeska

and a piece of sea life

on the hook for everything.

Save As Water

"the meeting-place of two seas."

For the desert nomads
oasis is a place-
holder for the placelessness
of paradise, exclusive
rights to stay the middle
of nowhere where the prose
flowing underground
and the light verse
falling from above
rhyme the garden green
with red hyacinths
for the travelers tempted
to move on, temples
beneath their tents.
             A body
of water, a scar of land,
echo of the mute
barrier between the calls
to prayer for the necks
bending back to look
up at islands rising
into a blank sky
level with the ground
on which one kneels to wash
the body with sand.

For Set

drives the waters back
to heaven, desert storms,
stirred up by Seth
annihilate the alien
akin to the prophet,
Setekh, turning his face
away to save his servant,
as Setesh, the face
always in, the back
of the head, slowly revolves
into view, confounding
sight.

     The fires too
forged in bodies of water
preserve salt, fires
that will never slake
the thirst of temples, much
less bodies driven
by fire, by thirst,
for water, land and bodies,
for rest always
blocked by the grave,
the crypt enwombs,
enwombs, worlds to come
a new body
forged in the likeness
of earth, largely water.

Setnet

Asea the *homo sapiens* among
us soon evaporate, condense above

as clouds, umbrella
of meta. The humans left
behind in cultures,
cro-Neanderthals in vexed
caves of Petri dis-

belief. Seas congeal,
suspend bridges, what gets through
stopped-up ears. A hand
overboard slows to a glove.
A leg retracts. A

production lists, for pyramid. The trade-
winds stage direction. *Exeunt* tows the wake.

2. Domestic

"imbecile candle"

I'm the a
taken for
granted self
made wick
without the
devilment
of outré stop
gap bridge
raised to the
nth degree
auto da auto
illuminations
for the wax is weak.

Dhow

Out here the affluenza of crude salt
Airs out, a spread
Of tradewind humors

The drone of an ambient language—
Flashfirefight—the power
Staked, an ante-

cedent modifier. Speak English.
Prepare to be boarded,
to come aboard all hope…

Bowsprit and Mast

The vernacular, a gentleman's sport
coat, soaked,
soiled for the sake of a lady's slip-
ons, clogs, mules, ends
up in the back of a second-hand store-
front as a vest—
plus a pair of pants fit for a pixie,
dwarf, troll,
who will come like Pinocchio's
nose
billowing like a narrowcast
chest
wrapped in the flag of a high
taken for tall

Barnacle and Patina

Call me drag

anchor *ab extra*
on the download

Tiresias 2.0
[x <u>and</u>—not <u>then</u>—y]

abridged. Call
update infected

attachment white
cell count plate-

let and own
house-mowed home

wanna-be hull.
Call me fresh

new coat of age
swamping blind pig

failed footage
cracked monocle.

Call me K

always on my way
to some benighted castle

uppermost prison
right of left

unstamped stockade
illegible keys.

Arapt

Oars at rest (backed-up
sloop), logged out.
blank screen, slack
sail (hedged canoe). Listless
list, save for sleepware
error—snore [sic]
snort—[sic] pitch, yaw-
n^{th} boot. Broken
link, a wake
hog-tied to this hand-held
(ahoy)—please God—heliport.

Pilot, Ltd.

aka ship to boat. Over-
board her middle née,
safety net her first Ms. No
last Mrs. The wheel her while,
feel of a massive underhandled minus.

Harbor's end in no time, and less
each time. She turns the wheel
over to the plot, elided little
__ in lieu of Captain.
He takes her here out to sea
and her? a slip, plus, the slip…

Gangplank of Sighs

Once upon a ship in the bottle
Ever after a popsicle stick O sticks   out

"twisted rudder"

my hands have got
one hand behind
                    my back

screw those bitches yelping fro'
"   " gold-diggers pawing for
                              some rocks

                              my other hand—
               my bridge loan—
floats my boat
          Ra-
          ward...

Punt Per Gondola

for Richard Pryor

A couple of poles taking a piss:
"Man, this water sure is cold."
"Deep too."

Versa Verso

washed ashore with driftwood, the underreported remains of a skiff, the brain, reportedly, sinks into sand, a sand hill with sandcastle, if not surfboard, aspirations, the skateboard of the mind, being said as a pouring-over, if not pored over, washes both, brain and mind, back into sand, out to sea where, perhaps, some port, if not some salvaging porter...

Maroon

On the other hand

real Kool-*ad*
hoc, abut men
running for exception, a
once-now-nonce, esq., briefly,
    a drawn shade
WANTED here, however
castaway shadow of the drowned—
    warriors walking underwater—

there, a shore
peppered with spent rounds

Library

I have always imagined that paradise will be a kind of library.

—Jorge Luis Borges

"Bully archives are the 'archive of archives', and are so vast in their claims that they often push other smaller topic-specific archives out of the way."

—Sameer Farook, *Speculative Archives Index*

Library Scientist

after Seshat

She
who scrivens
after 9—the
garden, flood, washed-
out lines, crops, etc.—re-
boots one
[deletes none]
spell 10
(cf. *Book of the Dead*)
opens the door to heaven
the

Mistress of the House of Books
and site manager of hotel/motel social media
files scrolls
catalogs spells
reserves heads
[disarticulated sky-s
over leftover
abbreviations
spoken for
by *ka*

aka *ba*

Fairy Godmother

grandfathers the wishes of the dead

sprinkles fairy

dust to dust

tombstone

tomb

shaft

burial

chamber

music somatics

sans semantics

the Lady of the House

notwithstood

weighs each soul—

light as a wafer

heavy as a book—

on her tongue

before another bloodbath

washes it down

where the elements

dissolve in acids

only she can stomach

China Today, momentous atom, another intelligent search for
intelligible death however charming our reservations for the outliers
West (e.g., Spokanes) and East (a terminal Hong Kong) of the
Red Blue White Book Everything the words nothing. Chiapas isn't
Kurdistan, much less dispersed Alawites, and so the fractional—not
to say factional—distinctions of the catalog prove useful, if quarky.
Still, the nano-dialectics of the crossroads—silk, climate, a wrong
turn, etc.—are not as predictable and thus reassuring as the mutually
massaged contradictions of—for example—the Mexican-cum-
District of Columbia-states, much less the up/down tribulations
of Al Mutanabbi Street, the imaginary of a broadside privy to
broadcasts with no air time for pages—which sometimes stick
together, sometimes go missing—to turn, tomorrow, to...to-....

A.D.A.M.

Acquisition

The political stances of the oceans—a *polis* sans people—are a function of their distances from the landlocked fulcrum and are measured per a battery of spoken prepositions (e.g., to, for, at...).

Development

Burned by the Braille performances of a blind sun, Ito Chuta, "one of the worst architects," deploys a red cloud, his umbrella and zeppelin, to carry him over the Ganges to tarry "on" the Bosphorus...

Access

A shrine a university gate, ways to—not of—the gods pouring out red al-Hadath as they pass overhead and below on their ways to other (uni-, poly-, di-) verses...

Management

Dead hand control means a legible acronym of irrecoverable or non-existent knowledge.

The Bully Archive

The everyday resurrections of the dead and living
not unlike invisible ships growing smaller and larger
as they sail into the glass bottles of open seas

bind the book and beyond divided by commerce
equals toe-tags carry the tag-lines to market
function irreducible to readings of the visible seen.

And the voices thrown overboard née overbody
borne as mistresses upon the waves they will never master
utter currency of off-shore arrears.

Thus exchange times the long division of geography
trade the remedy for accumulation of unique
copies. Vattermare, for instance, is and isn't

Mr. Alexandre, the hand and the hand inside the dummy,
the scandal of cadaver *lingua franca*, a cry
swept down river dragged for a drowned voice

adrift at sea for years before washing up
on the banks of New England. Here, Vattemare
and Mr. Alexandre find himself writ large

in uplift schemes, con games, and brutish cacophonies,
a dumb collection of semi-ingenious vessels,
 each a Noble *Homo erectus*, if not *Mercator sapiens*,

much less, nobleman. Here, a voice can find a mouth,
can offer to trade "a cast of the Venus de Milo"
for "an alligator," "a bull dog or a rattlesnake."

But V.'s appeal, eclipsed by M.'s showmanship,
can only raise an eyebrow or two, American hands
shoved deep into pockets far from French lapels.

Hence Mr. A. goes before to prepare and condense
an alphabet of omegas, to raise Montreal
as Boston, as Boston was to be a Paris,

to screen V. as V. screens A., each—seen—
blocking the scene, "two visages
under one hood," three facades—

an institute, a society, a library—to be
folded into one containment policy
but for the union of the territories

into Canada, one pre-emptive lumping
engulfing another as the sans serif of laissez-faire
logorrhea, an actuarial architecture.

Source and Target

The curse of *geniza* never exhumed—
merely excavated—condemns the old and new
anew, and once again the chosen few
find themselves delivered into the hands of many
strangers as they circle the earth and worlds
in the holding pattern of a paradise grove
under the stewardship of the hidden Imam
still forthcoming.

        Scuffles break out
with the local tillers who threaten to unionize.
Seconds in command, the set-aside gentrify
local flora, rebranded Eden Near.
Ground is broken for the sacred trash
art of state indigenous library.

Object Agent

after Sameer Farook and Lisa Samuels

Endowed by "the Canadian wife of a wealthy American merchant,"
the Haskell Free Library is less substrate made veneer, less a medium
corroding inscription from a trowel, brush or husband, than the soft
architectonics of "dis-cent," de-centered nexus of a common culture
evading the borderline meandering back and forth across the 45th
parallel, tracking the Buzzy Roys indifferent to the new checkpoints
and automatic weapons as he heads toward the pizzeria, a tangent
intercepted by Free World guards, Free Buzzy! placards jostling
above the rebels from Sanstead, Quebec and Derby Line, Vermont, a
petite soulevement through a line of flowerpots—an opening through
which Martha Haskell rises as a name evenly, with, history.....

The Speculative Archive

The carbon-12 footprint of a single fingernail
splits decision—decide to decide—or not—[14]decay
[13]stability and "life" the isotope of being

or pedestrian compound but for a pronounced
limp, tilt once the river freezes over
name expropriates every other proper brand

objects introjected and, flipped, catapulted against the subject
fortified however battered by the missing
pieces of an alleged puzzle. Ram face—

entry into exit from the maze of minotaur
lies: $14=12+13$, $14=25$, etc., base obfuscations
not unlike the flagged taxonomies of Linnaeus and Gray

against which an onomatophile and splitter, Rafinesque,
late of the Ottoman Empire, Italy and France,
a refugee loyal only to "the great laws…

symmetry, perpetuation, diversity, instability…,"
divines the principle of deviation no nomenclature
can arrest its pursuit of sheer proliferation no eye

can comprehend in its headlong hurry to see itself
before and after the interloping intercessors—
mirror, ocean, woman, etc.—to say nothing

of light, air. Rafinesque arrives at the Sound
shipwrecked, half-drowned, destitute, abandoned
("the deceit of women")—and then, a savior,

John Clifford, raises him like a prodigal, adopted, son,
a professorship, respect, however begrudging, of his peers,
a man among men, kin exchanged for kith

as he names begotten generations of reproductions
index gain and loss, algebra for numbers,
the reductive legacy of a Renaissance man

born centuries too late, and so, a naturalist
fit for keeping the books of nature, accounting
for what passes for not unlike the African

in the fit of birth-pangs, the Negro
wailing and gurgling as she emerges from her cis-womb
awashed in amniotic loss.

Objects in Exile

after Hema Amin

To market agoraphobia

every *e pluribus unum*

promotes a golden apple

from hidden quinces, Argan

fruit and, later, oranges,

a transfer protocol

collapsing three spheres into one

angelology: IT

hypertext simple mail file

fraud per Caliph Omar:

narrow the future into one book.

     ***

From the drop menu of the araf *firewall*

Q231 selects a flaming sword

as son—Q232 *en garde*

at the east gate of Error 404

as cherubim armed with dagger alifs

cut out the tongue, spilling

tongues onto an arid ground

cracking into harakat.

     ***

Inside the abandoned garden

that click-bait tree—

good cop/evil cop—

slumps under an overgrowth of burned books

sagging from the singed branches

of the first library closed indefinitely

for repairs to the studies under sheol *no more*

back-lit by sun than sun-lit moon

since the ways of the stars are not our star's.

                    ***

Outside on the plane of the planet

flat as the screens we scroll horizon-

horizon our long-distance carrier

neither delivers alerts to the ends of the earth

nor receives messages from the beginning of the world.

                                        At the precipice

some call waiting, leaning

over falls into the coma of epiphany,

deletes the comma at the end—

inserts a little i into the center—

of a sentence-period.

The D.I.Y. Archive

A wrapped lack addressed over and over
abhors itself the fundamental occultation
consigns orb-orbital orders to live

mummification: the museum appears as distance
per se, the promise of abolished horizons. Glass case law
edits unexpurgated malls strip science

down to séance. Call numbers interminable,
Special Collections sing from a shoreless far,
low-wire acts blow up the sky.

Going rogue assignments spots in, of, line,
pivot heads toward Launch Day, spines
face forward. Upright between the bookends of a century

a book of matches cannot be opened
by the tap tap of a cigarette
against the back of the other hand

as the palliative luxury of tobacco
leaves unfallen in a garden among the fields
supplant the dream of work after labor

when we will roll our own
or buy them from a church-front pharmacy
we may or may not own the smoke of e-

smokes stream live from the exhaust pipes
of nostrils as hands uncup and veils, dropped,
blow away like dreams woke. The Great God

Gumby sighs with pleasure in relief
against the white pages of his scrapbook
of Negroiana, would-be tear-sheets

that are only clippings of boxers, writers, politicians, etc.
while barbers, bellhops, butlers, porters, and postal clerks
never written up remain not unlike Gumby, Alexander,

the "smart dumbness" of consummate unconsummating men
palmed and fingered hither-thither by husbands and wives,
leftovers reserved for a future catalog called *Feast of Scraps*.

Jahiliyyah

after Thoth

Blue→green→gray
water footprints in profile point in one direction

imprint right east
heel a stride away

tamp down point step over nonpoint
left-handedness

basin groundwaters the lake of books
burns forever

thought intelligence knowledge wisdom logic
reason measure writing magic secrets

ibis- and baboon-headed
judge and court stenographer

weigh and record the souls on/in file
petroglyphs of underground

petroleum deposits

placemakers

make way for the wayfarers of the desert
sail across the sands all thanks to Ra

steady at their backs→billowing chests
pull out mobiles

click on trees the animé of life
save as oars

Burn the Book of Life

Still I follow, in burning these books, the model of leading masters who are to be emulated, whose guidance is embraced, and whose fire is sought by the dim-sighted.

Abu Hayyan al-Tawhidi

Rumored wildfires—a Christian mob, a harbor of burning ships, the book to claymore books moot—spread to forests after immolating tree lines—Alexandria, Antioch, Ashurbanipal...

Ticknor and Smithson notwithstanding, "the librarian has never been able to bend his patron to his purpose," and thus adult education is poorly served by this public fount of voracious omniscience which deigns to "irrigate the surrounding wastelands of human ignorance" but hoards its nectar while drenching the plains, waters rising to flood proportions, and Noah a Cloud above no land or water...

burn the book of life

and the cuneiforms solidify in the purifying fires of papyri, leather, wax

burn the book of life

and the last three books of a Sibyl must be purchased at great cost a
complete collection

burn the book of life

and the northern wall of the incinerated Persepolis Fortification
Archive collapses onto spared clay tablets, encaving the sleepers long
before Ephesus

burn the book of life

and the Trial of the Talmud ends in conviction as the scroll burns
and/but "the letters fly up in the air"

burn the book of life

and Abdul Kader Haidara transfers manuscripts from the Ahmed
Bata Institute of Higher Learning and Islamic Research to locations
unknown, a metaphor eluding the fleeing literalists of Ansar Dine

burn the book of life

and the kneeling drink from a Tigris black with ink

After Word Read Digest

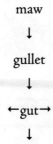

maw
↓
gullet
↓
←gut→
↓

Tyrone Williams teaches literature and theory at Xavier University in Cincinnati, Ohio. He is the author of several chapbooks and five books of poetry: *c.c., On Spec, The Hero Project of the Century, Adventures of Pi* and *Howell*. A limited-edition art project, *Trump l'oeil*, was published by Hostile Books in 2017. His website is at http://home.earthlink.net/~suspend/